This Book
Belongs to:

MY FIRST ANIMAL ACTIVITY BOOK

FOR KIDS 3-5

Written by Krissy Bonning-Gould
Illustrations by Robin Boyer

ROCKRIDGE
PRESS

To my favorite "animals," Sawyer, Priscilla, and J.C.
—K.B.G.

Interior and Cover Designer: Scott Petrower
Art Producer: Sara Feinstein
Editor: Laura Bryn Sisson
Production Editor: Mia Moran
Illustrations © 2020 Robin Boyer

ISBN: Print 978-1-64611-249-4
RO

Animal Adventure!

Whether going on safari, sliding with penguins, visiting the dog park, or milking the cows, a fun-filled animal adventure awaits in the pages ahead. You'll find five types of engaging animal-themed activities: coloring pages, dot-to-dots, mazes, matching games, and spot-the-difference puzzles.

Activities increase in difficulty as the book goes on, but all are perfectly suited for children aged 3 to 5. After a quick explanation of each type of activity, your child will be off on an exciting animal adventure!

A Little Snack

Home, Sweet Home!

Draw a line to match each pet to its home. Then color them in.

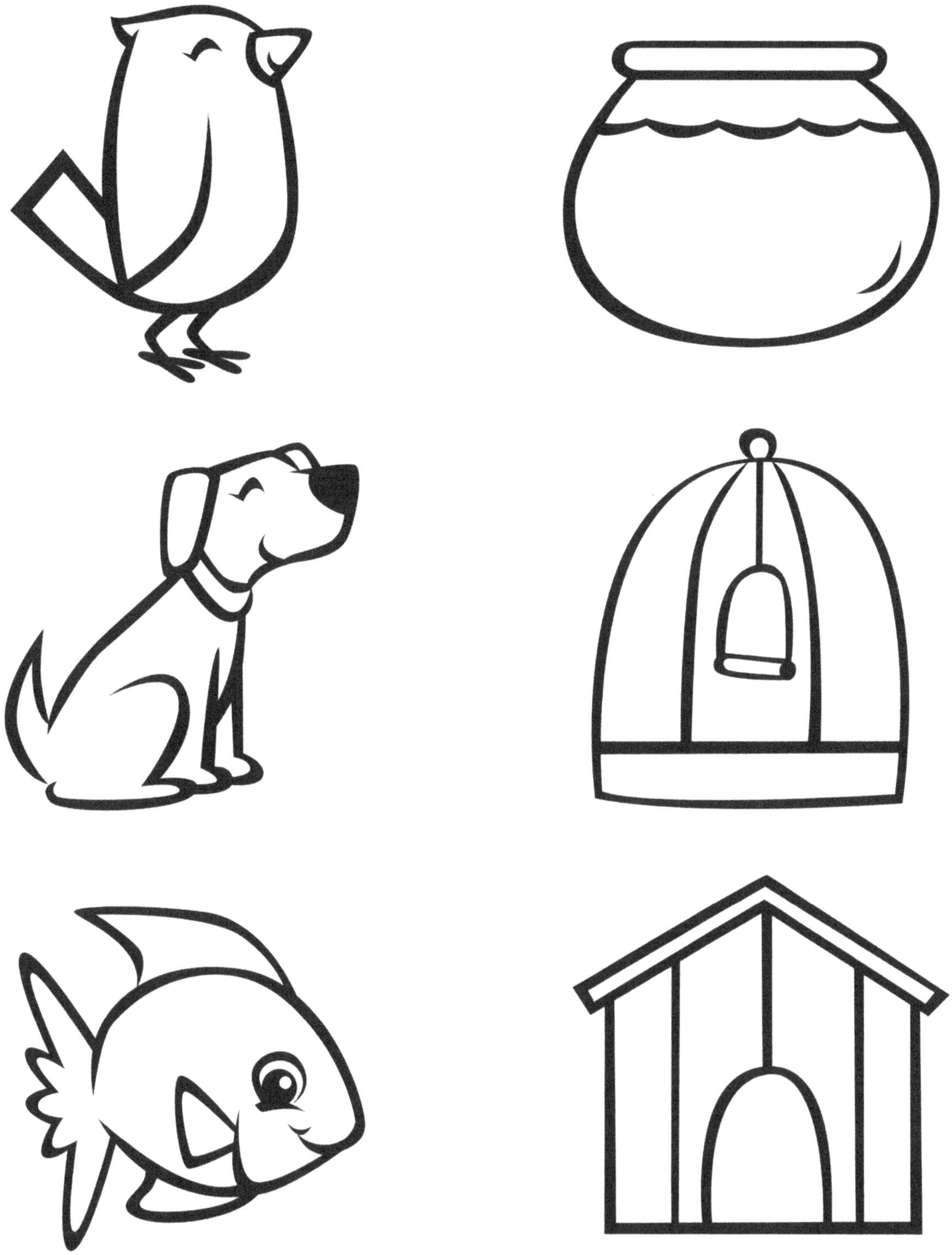

See page 80 for the answer key!

Splish-Splash!

Bones Are Best

Connect the dots to show which animal likes to chew a bone. Start with 1 and go in order. Then trace the letters to spell its name, and color the picture.

See page 80 for the answer key!

Back to the Burrow

Help our gopher friend get home for dinner.
Steer clear of worms, and stay on the paths.

See page 80 for the answer key!

Ready to Play?

Farm Fun!

A farm is a busy place! Find **3** differences between the two farm pictures, then color the images.

See page 80 for the answer key!

A Splendid Spiral

Forest Animal Families

Draw a line to match each forest animal to its family.
Then color them in.

See page 81 for the answer key!

Gracefully Gliding

Connect the dots to show the animal that glides gracefully across the pond. Start at 1 and go in order. Then trace the letters to spell its name, and color the picture.

See page 81 for the answer key!

All Ears

Rat Race

Can you help the pet rat get to their rat friend at the top of the cage? Be careful to stay on the paths.

See page 81 for the answer key!

A Happy Hedgehog

Monkey-ing Around

Most monkeys live in trees. Find **3** differences between the two pictures, then color the images.

See page 81 for the answer key!

Fronts & Backs

Draw a line to match each animal's front half to its back half. Then color them in.

See page 82 for the answer key!

Soaking Up the Sun

Home On-the-Go!

Connect the dots to show which animal always carries its home. Start at 1 and go in order. Then trace the letters to spell its name, and color the picture.

See page 82 for the answer key!

Wonderful Wings!

Busy Buzzy Bee

Help the worker bee get to the queen bee.
Steer clear of the sticky honey, and stay on the paths!

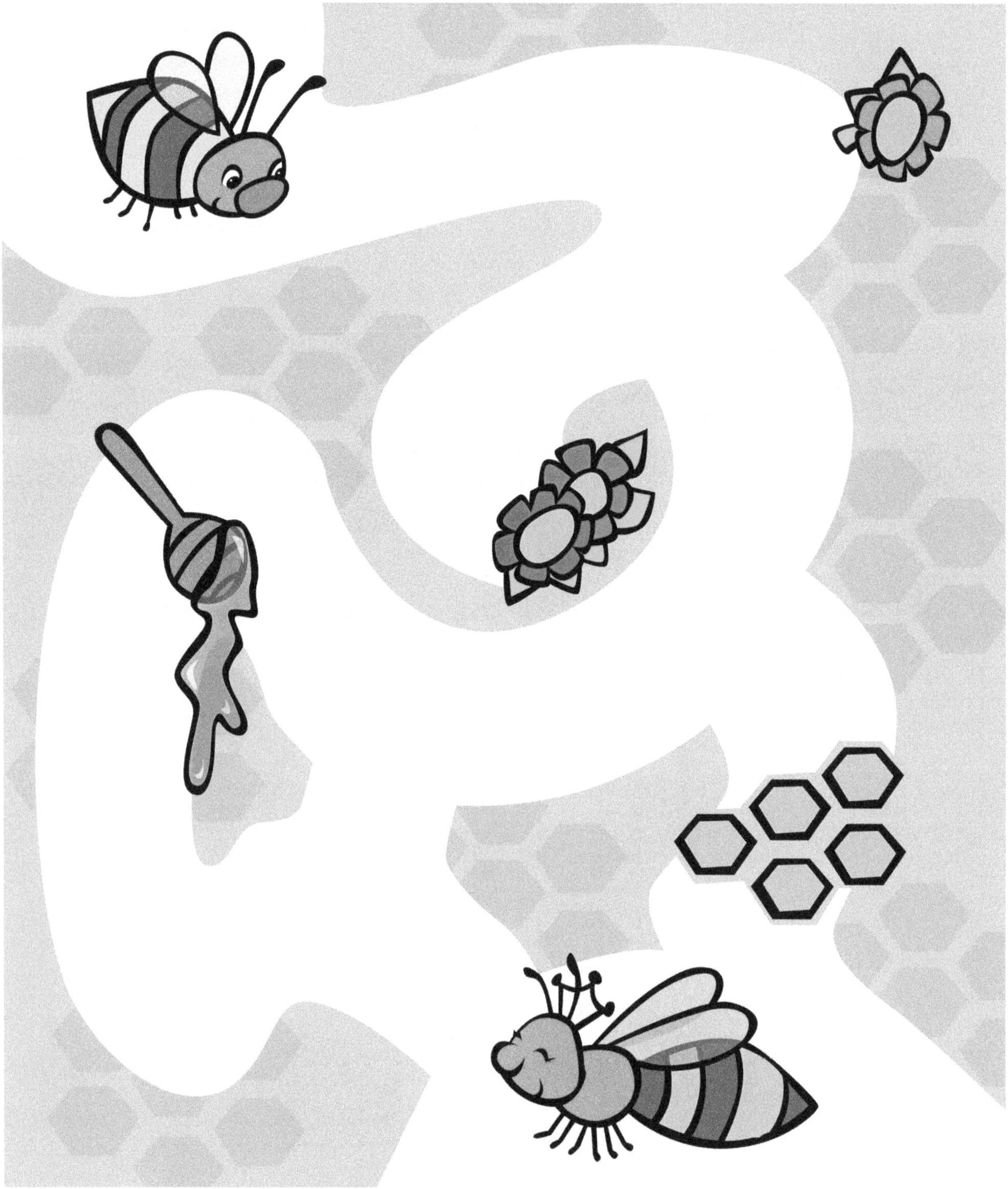

See page 82 for the answer key!

Warm & Snug

A mommy kangaroo carries her baby in her pouch. Find **3** differences between the two kangaroo pictures, then color the images.

See page 82 for the answer key!

Hee-Haw!

Pattern Play

Draw a line to match each animal to its pattern.
Then color them in.

See page 83 for the answer key!

Whale Watching

Snap, Snap!

Connect the dots to show the animal that has claws. Start at 1 and go in order. Then trace the letters to spell its name, and color the picture.

See page 83 for the answer key!

Flyswatter Frenzy!

Help the fly get to the picnic. Watch out for the flyswatters, and stay on the path!

See page 83 for the answer key!

Funny Fish School

Did you know that fish who swim together are called a "school" of fish?
Find **4** differences between the two pictures, then color the images.

See page 83 for the answer key!

Big Hippo Bath

Barnyard Babies

Draw a line to match each farm animal with its baby. Then color them in.

See page 84 for the answer key!

Llama Mama Love

Nesting

Connect the dots to show which animal keeps her eggs safe in a nest. Start with 1 and go in order. Then trace the letters to spell its name, and color the picture.

See page 84 for the answer key!

Squirrel Scramble

Help the squirrel get the acorn to their stash of acorns. Steer clear of the other squirrels who want to steal it, and don't cross any tree branches or leave the path.

See page 84 for the answer key!

Pelican Patrol

Tropical Tree Dweller

Iguanas love being in the trees! Find **5** differences between the two iguana pictures, then color the images.

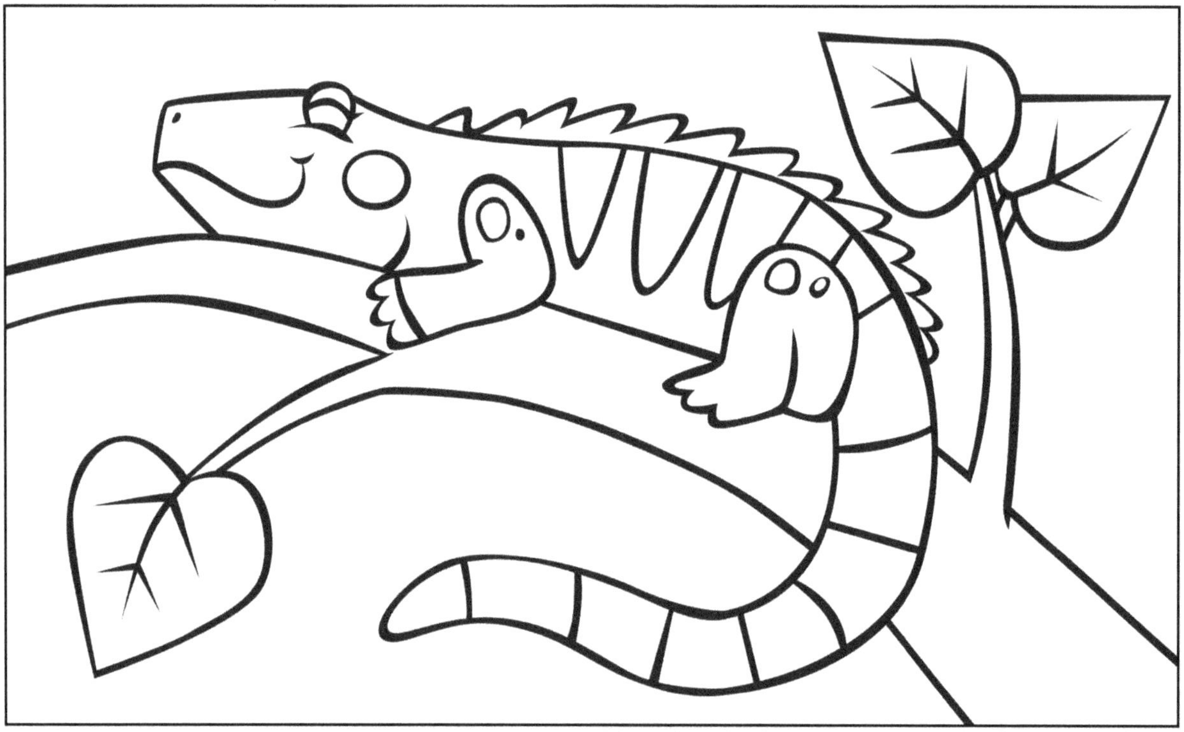

See page 84 for the answer key!

Miss Lady Daisy

Help Them Home

Draw a line to match each animal to its home.
Then color them in.

See page 85 for the answer key!

Slow & Steady

Connect the dots to reveal the slowest animal in the rainforest. Start at 1 and go in order. Then trace the letters to spell its name, and color the picture.

sloth

See page 85 for the answer key!

Parrot Pals

Slip & Slide!

Penguins sometimes slide on their bellies to get around. Help this penguin slide along the icy path to join their penguin friends. Don't cross any snowflakes!

See page 85 for the answer key!

Fishbowl Friend

Pond Party

So much goes on in a pond! Find **5** differences between the two pond pictures, then color the images.

See page 85 for the answer key!

Which Tail?

Draw a line to match each animal to its tail. Then color them in.

See page 86 for the answer key!

Just Hanging Around

A Sweet Treat

Connect the dots to see which tiny animal loves a sweet treat. Start at 1 and go in order. Then trace the letters to spell its name, and color the picture.

See page 86 for the answer key!

WHOO Are You?

Panda Paradise

Help the panda get to its favorite food—bamboo! Watch out for rocks and the river, and don't leave the path.

See page 86 for the answer key!

Sunny Day

This horse loves the warm sunshine and grassy pasture.
Find **5** differences between the two pictures, then color the images.

See page 86 for the answer key!

Cock-A-Doodle-Doo!

Who's Hungry?

Draw a line to match each animal to its food. Then color them in.

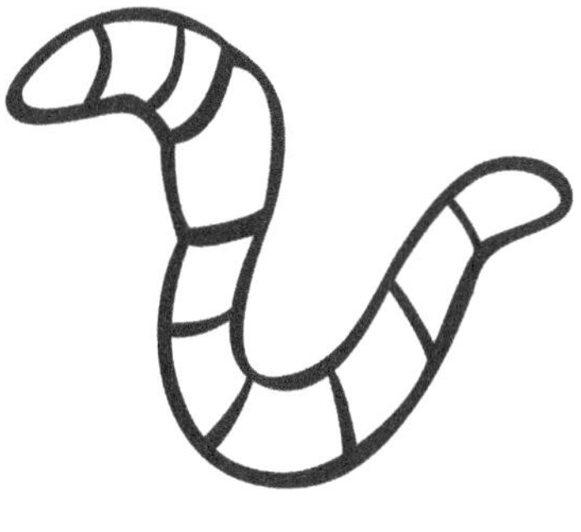

See page 87 for the answer key!

Desert Stroll

Connect the dots to reveal the animal that can walk a long way in the desert. Start at 1 and go in order. Then trace the letters to spell its name, and color the picture.

camel

See page 87 for the answer key!

Muddy Fun!

Getting muddy helps pigs stay cool in hot weather. Help this pig get to the mud pit. Watch out for the other farm animals, and stay on the paths!

See page 87 for the answer key!

Peck, Peck, Peck

Welcome to the Pet Store!

Have you ever visited a pet store? Find **5** differences between these two pictures, then color the images.

See page 87 for the answer key!

Curious Creatures

Farm Animal Shadows

Draw a line to match each farm animal to its shadow.
Then color them in.

See page 88 for the answer key!

Hitching a Ride

Connect the dots to show the animal that carries her baby on her back. Start at 1 and go in order. Then trace the letters to spell its name, and color the picture.

koala

See page 88 for the answer key!

Pretty as a Peacock!

Ant Hunt

Can you help the anteater find some ants for dinner?
Watch out for the branches and rocks, and stay on the paths.

See page 88 for the answer key!

The Horse of the Sea

Kitty Cafe

Did you know that some coffee shops welcome cats? Find **7** differences between the two kitty cafe pictures, then color the images.

See page 88 for the answer key!

Habitat Homes

A "habitat" is a place where an animal lives.
Draw a line to match each animal to its habitat. Then color them in.

See page 89 for the answer key!

Amazing Octopus

Sss . . . Slithering in the Sand

Connect the dots to show the animal slithering in the sandy desert. Start with A and go in alphabetical order. Then trace the letters to spell its name, and color the picture.

snake

See page 89 for the answer key!

Gobble, Gobble

Dog Park Dash!

Help the dog get through the busy dog park and back to their owner. Watch out for the other dogs, and stay on the paths!

See page 89 for the answer key!

Silly Safari

Let's go on safari! Find **7** differences between the two safari pictures, then color the images.

See page 89 for the answer key!

The Forest in Fall

Find My Feet!

Draw a line to match each animal to its missing legs and feet.
Then color them in.

See page 90 for the answer key!

Jungle Jam!

Grass Grazers

Connect the dots to show the bird that spends more time in grass than in trees. Start at 1 and go in order. Then trace the letters to spell its name, and color it in.

See page 90 for the answer key!

Time to Milk the Cows!

Help the farmer get to her cows for milking time. Steer clear of the corn and scarecrow, and stay on the paths.

See page 90 for the answer key!

Desert Armadillos

Happy Hamsters

Pet hamsters love to run and play. Find **8** differences between these two pictures, then color the images.

See page 90 for the answer key!

Lots of Spots

Making Tracks

Draw a line to match each animal to its tracks. Then color them in.

See page 91 for the answer key!

Howl!

Connect the dots to show which animal howls to communicate with others. Start at A and go in alphabetical order. Then trace the letters to spell its name, and color the picture.

See page 91 for the answer key!

Lion Lunch

It's lunchtime at the zoo! Help the zookeeper take lunch to the lions. Walk around the other zoo animals, and stay on the paths.

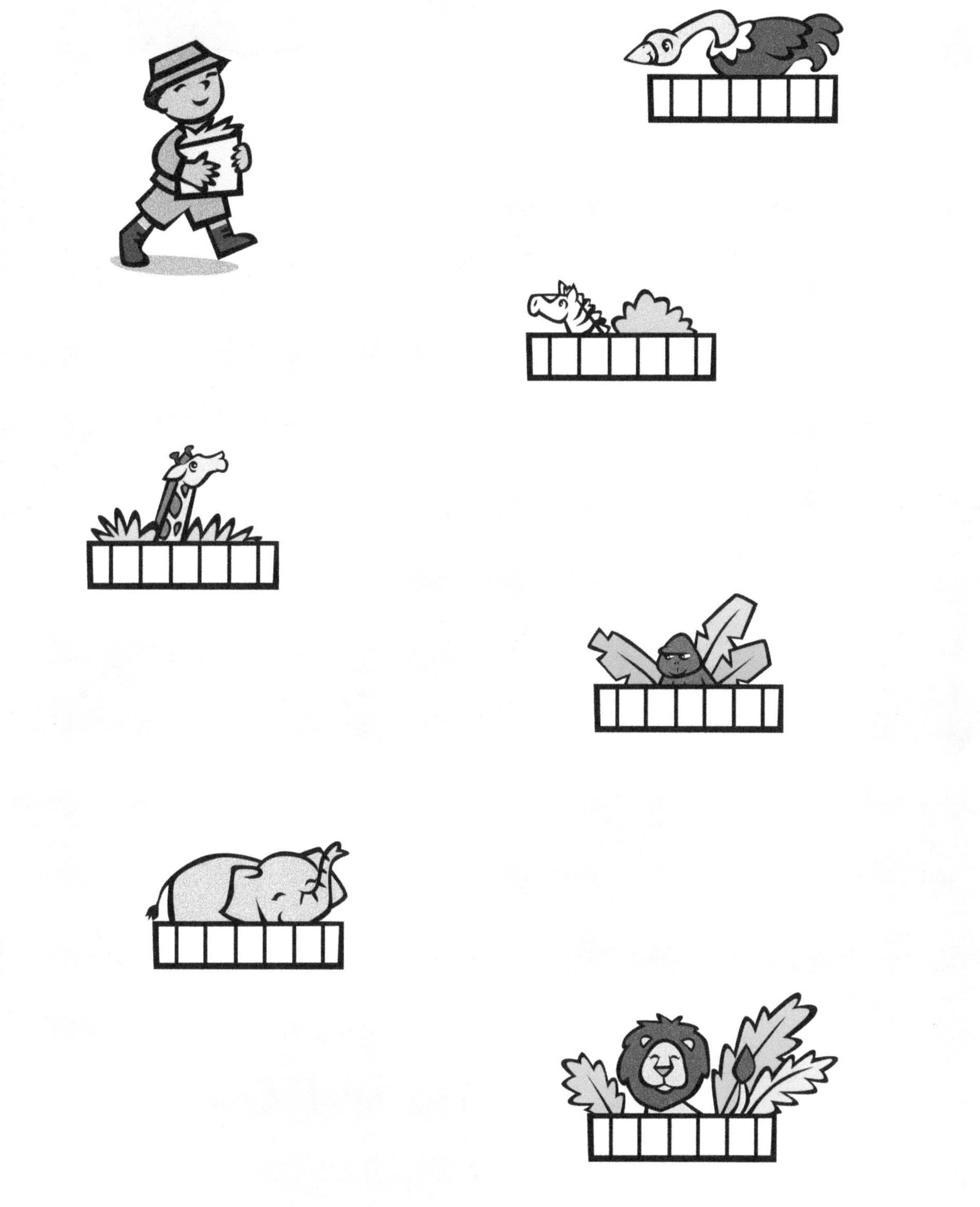

See page 91 for the answer key!

Tiger Time

Sunflower Fun

Do you know which animals love sunflowers? Insects! Find **8** differences between the two sunflower pictures, then color the images.

See page 91 for the answer key!

Answer Key

Home, Sweet Home!
Draw a line to match each pet to its home. Then color them in.
See page 80 for the answer key!
3

Page 3

Bones Are Best
Connect the dots to show which animal likes to chew a bone. Start with 1 and go in order. Then trace the letters to spell its name, and color the picture.
dog
See page 80 for the answer key!
5

Page 5

Back to the Burrow
Help our gopher friend get home for dinner. Steer clear of worms, and stay on the paths.
See page 80 for the answer key!
6

Page 6

Farm Fun!
A farm is a busy place! Find 3 differences between the two farm pictures, then color the images.
See page 80 for the answer key!
8

Page 8

Answer Key

Forest Animal Families
Draw a line to match each forest animal to its family. Then color them in.
See page 81 for the answer key!
10

Page 10

Gracefully Gliding
Connect the dots to show the animal that glides gracefully across the pond. Start at 1 and go in order. Then trace the letters to spell its name, and color the picture.
1
2
3
4
5
6
7
8
9
10
swan
See page 81 for the answer key!
11

Page 11

Rat Race
Can you help the pet rat get to their rat friend at the top of the cage? Be careful to stay on the paths.
See page 81 for the answer key!
13

Page 13

Monkey-ing Around
Most monkeys live in trees. Find 3 differences between the two pictures, then color the images.
See page 81 for the answer key!
15

Page 15

Answer Key

Fronts & Backs

Draw a line to match each animal's front half to its back half. Then color them in.

See page 82 for the answer key!

16

Page 16

Home On-the-Go!

Connect the dots to show which animal always carries its home. Start at 1 and go in order. Then trace the letters to spell its name, and color the picture.

See page 82 for the answer key!

18

Page 18

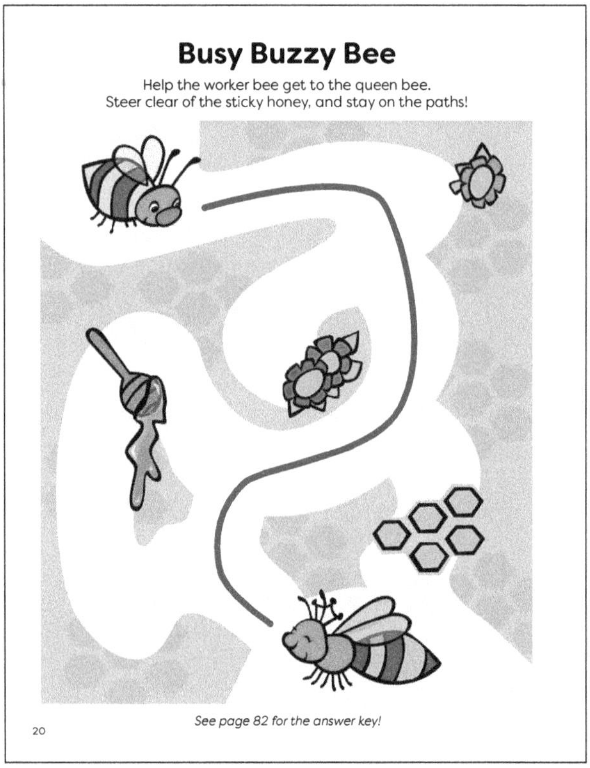

Busy Buzzy Bee

Help the worker bee get to the queen bee. Steer clear of the sticky honey, and stay on the paths!

See page 82 for the answer key!

20

Page 20

Warm & Snug

A mommy kangaroo carries her baby in her pouch. Find **3** differences between the two kangaroo pictures, then color the images.

See page 82 for the answer key!

21

Page 21

Answer Key

Pattern Play
Draw a line to match each animal to its pattern. Then color them in.
See page 83 for the answer key!
23

Page 23

Snap, Snap!
Connect the dots to show the animal that has claws. Start at 1 and go in order. Then trace the letters to spell its name, and color the picture.
1
2
3
4
5
6
7
8
9
10
11
12
13
14
15
crab
See page 83 for the answer key!
25

Page 25

Flyswatter Frenzy!
Help the fly get to the picnic. Watch out for the flyswatters, and stay on the path!
See page 83 for the answer key!
26

Page 26

Funny Fish School
Did you know that fish who swim together are called a "school" of fish? Find 4 differences between the two pictures, then color the images.
See page 83 for the answer key!
27

Page 27

Answer Key

Barnyard Babies

Draw a line to match each farm animal with its baby. Then color them in.

See page 84 for the answer key!

29

Page 29

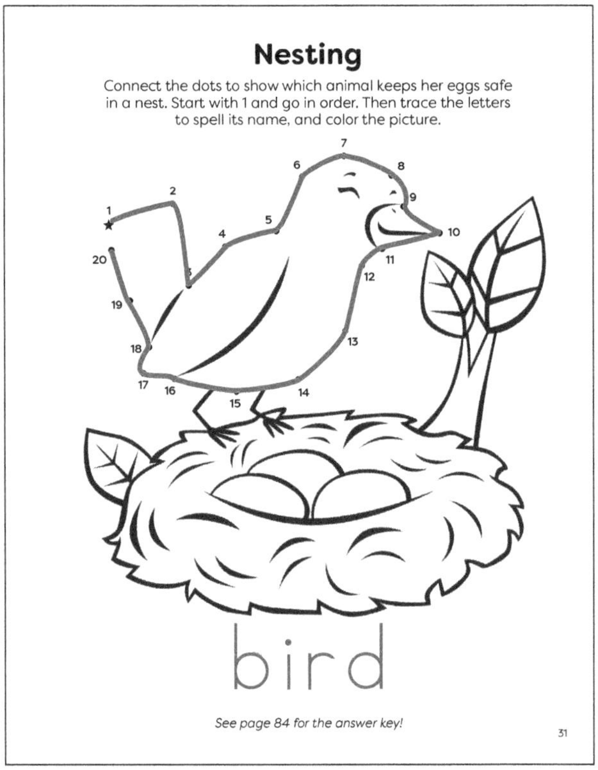

Nesting

Connect the dots to show which animal keeps her eggs safe in a nest. Start with 1 and go in order. Then trace the letters to spell its name, and color the picture.

bird

See page 84 for the answer key!

31

Page 31

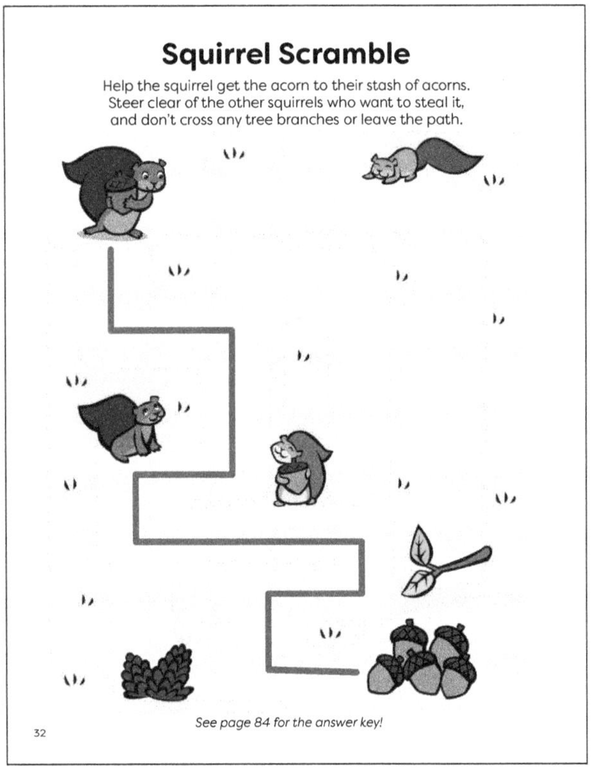

Squirrel Scramble

Help the squirrel get the acorn to their stash of acorns. Steer clear of the other squirrels who want to steal it, and don't cross any tree branches or leave the path.

32

See page 84 for the answer key!

Page 32

Tropical Tree Dweller

Iguanas love being in the trees! Find **5** differences between the two iguana pictures, then color the images.

34

See page 84 for the answer key!

Page 34

Answer Key

Help Them Home

Draw a line to match each animal to its home. Then color them in.

See page 85 for the answer key!

Page 36

Slow & Steady

Connect the dots to reveal the slowest animal in the rainforest. Start at 1 and go in order. Then trace the letters to spell its name, and color the picture.

See page 85 for the answer key!

Page 37

Slip & Slide!

Penguins sometimes slide on their bellies to get around. Help this penguin slide along the icy path to join their penguin friends. Don't cross any snowflakes!

See page 85 for the answer key!

Page 39

Pond Party

So much goes on in a pond! Find **5** differences between the two pond pictures, then color the images.

See page 85 for the answer key!

Page 41

Answer Key

Which Tail?

Draw a line to match each animal to its tail. Then color them in.

See page 86 for the answer key!

42

Page 42

A Sweet Treat

Connect the dots to see which tiny animal loves a sweet treat. Start at 1 and go in order. Then trace the letters to spell its name, and color the picture.

See page 86 for the answer key!

44

Page 44

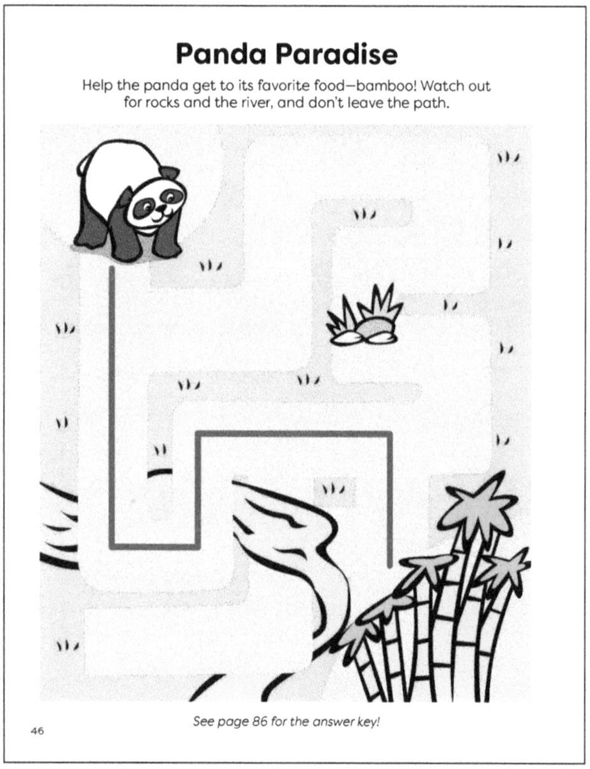
Panda Paradise

Help the panda get to its favorite food—bamboo! Watch out for rocks and the river, and don't leave the path.

See page 86 for the answer key!

46

Page 46

Sunny Day

This horse loves the warm sunshine and grassy pasture. Find **5** differences between the two pictures, then color the images.

See page 86 for the answer key!

47

Page 47

Answer Key

Who's Hungry?
Draw a line to match each animal to its food. Then color them in.
See page 87 for the answer key!
49

Page 49

Desert Stroll
Connect the dots to reveal the animal that can walk a long way in the desert. Start at 1 and go in order. Then trace the letters to spell its name, and color the picture.
camel
See page 87 for the answer key!
50

Page 50

Muddy Fun!
Getting muddy helps pigs stay cool in hot weather. Help this pig get to the mud pit. Watch out for the other farm animals, and stay on the paths!
See page 87 for the answer key!
51

Page 51

Welcome to the Pet Store!
Have you ever visited a pet store? Find 5 differences between these two pictures, then color the images.
Pets!
Pets
See page 87 for the answer key!
53

Page 53

Answer Key

Farm Animal Shadows
Draw a line to match each farm animal to its shadow.
Then color them in.
See page 88 for the answer key!
55

Page 55

Hitching a Ride
Connect the dots to show the animal that carries her baby on her back. Start at 1 and go in order. Then trace the letters to spell its name, and color the picture.
koala
56
See page 88 for the answer key!

Page 56

Ant Hunt
Can you help the anteater find some ants for dinner?
Watch out for the branches and rocks, and stay on the paths.
58
See page 88 for the answer key!

Page 58

Kitty Cafe
Did you know that some coffee shops welcome cats? Find 7 differences between the two kitty cafe pictures, then color the images.
60
See page 88 for the answer key!

Page 60

Answer Key

Habitat Homes
A "habitat" is a place where an animal lives.
Draw a line to match each animal to its habitat. Then color them in.
See page 89 for the answer key!
61

Page 61

Sss . . . Slithering in the Sand
Connect the dots to show the animal slithering in the sandy desert.
Start with A and go in alphabetical order. Then trace the letters
to spell its name, and color the picture.
snake
See page 89 for the answer key!
63

Page 63

Dog Park Dash!
Help the dog get through the busy dog park and back to their owner.
Watch out for the other dogs, and stay on the paths!
See page 89 for the answer key!
65

Page 65

Silly Safari
Let's go on safari! Find 7 differences between
the two safari pictures, then color the images.
See page 89 for the answer key!
66

Page 66

Answer Key

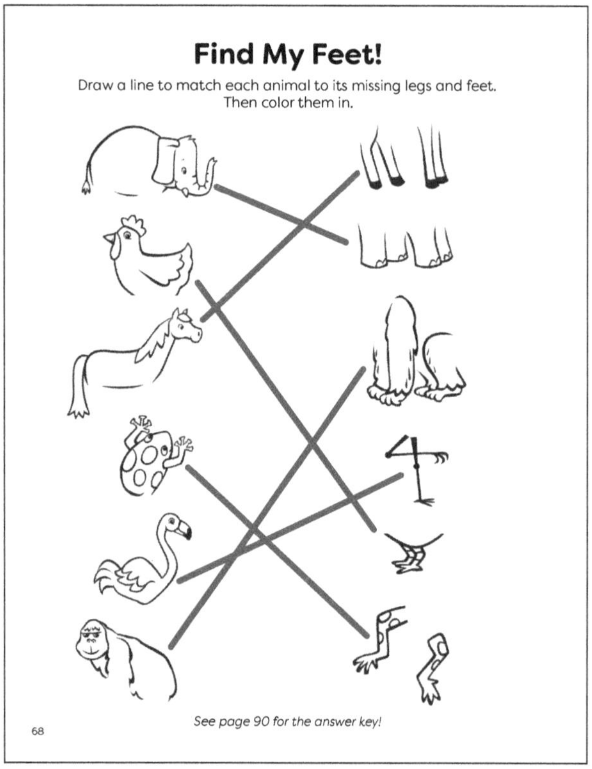

Find My Feet!
Draw a line to match each animal to its missing legs and feet. Then color them in.
See page 90 for the answer key!
68

Page 68

Grass Grazers
Connect the dots to show the bird that spends more time in grass than in trees. Start at 1 and go in order. Then trace the letters to spell its name, and color it in.
quail
See page 90 for the answer key!
70

Page 70

Time to Milk the Cows!
Help the farmer get to her cows for milking time. Steer clear of the corn and scarecrow, and stay on the paths.
See page 90 for the answer key!
71

Page 71

Happy Hamsters
Pet hamsters love to run and play. Find 8 differences between these two pictures, then color the images.
See page 90 for the answer key!
73

Page 73

Answer Key

Making Tracks

Draw a line to match each animal to its tracks. Then color them in.

See page 91 for the answer key!

Page 75

Howl!

Connect the dots to show which animal howls to communicate with others. Start at A and go in alphabetical order. Then trace the letters to spell its name, and color the picture.

See page 91 for the answer key!

Page 76

Lion Lunch

It's lunchtime at the zoo! Help the zookeeper take lunch to the lions. Walk around the other zoo animals, and stay on the paths.

See page 91 for the answer key!

Page 77

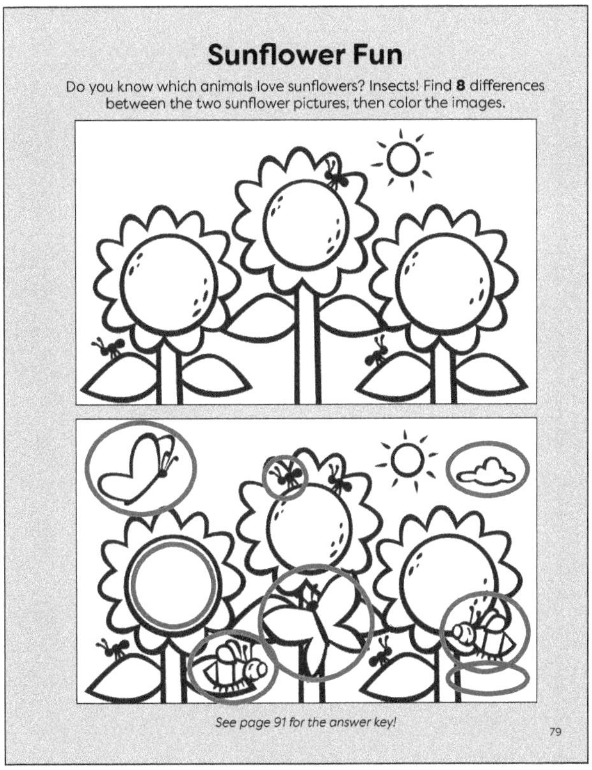

Sunflower Fun

Do you know which animals love sunflowers? Insects! Find **8** differences between the two sunflower pictures, then color the images.

See page 91 for the answer key!

Page 79

About the Author

Krissy Bonning-Gould is a former art teacher with a master's degree in K-12 Art Education turned full-time blogging mama. Upon becoming a mom, Krissy founded *B-Inspired Mama* simply as a creative outlet; however, it ignited a passion within her for blogging and helping fellow moms. Over the past ten years, between pregnancies and playdates for her children, Sawyer, Priscilla, and J. C., Krissy immersed herself in blogging, social media, and content marketing to grow B-InspiredMama.com into an extensive resource of inspiration for kids' crafts, learning fun, kid-friendly recipes, and creative parenting. Follow her fun via email at B-InspiredMama.com/subscribe and on social media by following @BInspiredMama on Twitter and Instagram, Pinterest.com/BInspiredMama, Facebook.com/BInspiredMama, and Facebook.com/SensoryActivitiesforKids. Aside from blogging, Krissy has also authored three toddler activity books, *The Outdoor Toddler Activity Book*, *The Rainy Day Toddler Activity Book*, and *Toddler Activities Made Easy*, available in bookstores nationwide and online.

About the Illustrator

Robin Boyer started her career path with a summer art and design program at the Art Institute of Chicago, then attended Alma College where she earned her Bachelor of Fine Arts in design and illustration. She started out as a graphic designer and in-house illustrator for a publishing company before changing her attentions to freelance illustration. She has been a freelance illustrator for over 17 years and continues to illustrate for various children's book publishers around the world. She loves the variety of projects that she has had the opportunity to work on. From board books to hidden pictures and everything in between, each project allows her to use her creativity and bring pictures to words. When she is not busy drawing away in her studio, she is cheering on her two children in their various sports and school activities and enjoying life in a west Michigan beach town.

Congratulations!

____

has finished this activity book.

Great job!

CPSIA information can be obtained
at www.ICGtesting.com
Printed in the USA
JSHW011455210420
5205JS00001B/3

9 781646 112494